Living
in the
Shadows

Rev. Larry Detruf

ASA Publishing Corporation
1285 N. Telegraph Rd., PMB #376, Monroe, Michigan 48162
An Accredited Publishing House with the BBB
www.asapublishingcorporation.com

All Rights Reserved. No part of this publication may be reproduced, stored in a retrieval system or transmitted in any form or by any means electronic, mechanical, photocopying, recording or otherwise, without the prior written permission of the publisher. Author/writer rights to "Freedom of Speech" protected by and with the "1st Amendment" of the Constitution of the United States of America. This is a work of non-fiction Christian educational belief. Any resemblance to actual events, locales, person living or deceased that is not related to the author's literacy is entirely coincidental.

With this title/copyrights page, the reader is notified that the publisher does not assume, and expressly disclaims any obligation to obtain and/or include any other information other than that provided by the author except with permission. Any belief system, promotional motivations, including but not limited to the use of non-fictional/fictional characters and/or characteristics of this book, are within the boundaries of the author's own creativity in order to reflect the nature and concept of the book. Unless otherwise indicated, all scripture quotations are taken from standard Christian biblical studies such as KJV, NKJV, NIV, RSV and such alike.

Any and all vending sales and distribution not permitted without full book cover and this copyrights page.

Copyrights©2019 Rev. Larry Detruf, All Rights Reserved
Book Title: Living in the Shadows
Date Published: 01.02.2020 / Edition 1 *Trade Paperback*
Book ID: ASAPCID2380798
ISBN: 978-1-946746-65-8
Library of Congress Cataloging-in-Publication Data

This book was published in the United States of America.
Great State of Michigan

Table of Contents

Preface 1

Chapter One
Living in the Shadow of Sin 9
    Presumptuous Sin 11
    Other Men's Sins 11
    Faithless Sin 13
    Ignorant Sin 14
    Willful Sin 15
    Sin of Omission 16
    Shedding the Shadow of Sin 19

Chapter Two
Living in the Shadow of Guilt 21
    Shedding the Shadow of Guilt 26

Chapter Three
Living in the Shadow of Fear 29
    Fear is not God's plan for our lives 30
    Fear is contagious 31
    Fear is natural 33

Most fears are borrowed 34
There is always an 'exit' from fear 36
Shedding the Shadow of Fear 39

Chapter Four

Living in the Shadow of Doubt 41
   Fear 43
   Divided loyalties 44
   Lack of focus 45
   Poor choices 47
   Distractions 48
   Shedding the Shadow of Doubt 51

Chapter Five

Living in the Shadow of Bitterness 53
   Shedding the Shadow of Bitterness 60
   Presumptuous Sin 0
   Presumptuous Sin 0
   Presumptuous Sin 0
   Questionnaires 0

Chapter Six

Living in the Shadow of Unforgiveness 63
   Shedding the Shadow of Unforgiveness 70

Chapter Seven

Living in the Shadow of Greed/Covetousness 73

Shedding the Shadow of Greed/Covetousness 80

Chapter Eight

Living in the Shadow of Lust 83

Steps to full surrender and victory 92

Shedding the Shadow of Lust 94

Chapter Nine

Living in the Shadow of Death 97

Everyone dies 100

Fear of death is bondage 101

Not everyone dies 'on time' 102

Life outlasts death 103

We must be ready 105

The ultimate goal 106

Shedding the Shadow of Death 108

Chapter Ten

Living in the Shadow of the Almighty 111

Dwell 112

Trust 112

Truth 113

Love 114
Call 116
Satisfy 117
Dwelling in the Shadow of the Almighty 118

PREFACE

When God calls us to draw near, and serve Him with our lives, we never really know where that call will take us. I never dreamed it would be a call to sell everything and move to Florida to prepare for full time Pastoral Ministry! I had no idea how many people He would use along the way to shape who I would become, and what I would be doing; I was totally unprepared for the journey He had set me on. This small book is the result of the love, the instruction, the correction (and sometimes the tolerance), and the support and encouragement they provided. There is a saying that "everything begins at home", and I certainly know that to be true in my life.

When my wife Sandy and I got married, neither of us had any clue that our future would be in Christian Ministry; we had no intention of selling our home, or of moving to Florida to continue my education; and we had absolutely no plans to move to Michigan to serve in Pastoral Ministry. Sandy gave up her dream of becoming a teacher, so that we could pursue the call God had placed upon our lives. My prayer for every person called to full time ministry, is that they would have a spouse as supportive and committed as mine. Thank you, Sandy, I truly could not, and probably would not, have done it without you!

My daughter Corrie was 7 years old when we packed her an our few remaining belongings into our station wagon, leaving all her friends and family behind. Then, just two years later, we repeated the process, and took a call to Pastor the First Church of God in Monroe, Michigan. She lived the next nine years of her childhood in the 'Fishbowl', under the label, and often the unfair and unrealistic expectations that accompanied being the "Pastor's kid"! She endured the disappointment of interrupted plans, and family night events because of Church, and congregational needs and emergencies. Thank you, Corrie, for loving and supporting your Dad!

My Pastor, Foster Brock, Jr. greatly shaped not only my understanding, but also the practical passion and exercise of Pastoral Ministry. I will never be able to convey how much his mentorship has meant to me, and to those I have ministered to!

All of the Professors and students at Warner Southern College in Lake Wales, Florida were instrumental in one way or another, and influenced and helped shape me for the ministry God was calling me to. Sandy and I often refer to those years as our 'wilderness experience'; but it was a journey worth taking!

The congregation at the First Church of God in Monroe, Michigan took a chance on a green (and occasionally stupid) young preacher, and for thirty-two years loved, endured, forgave, encouraged and supported me. Thank you for all you did to make long term ministry possible!

My very dear, and unexpected friends, Rev. Dr. Robert O. Dulin, Jr. and his sweet wife Alruthus came into my life late in ministry, when he served as the Regional Pastor in the Church of God in Michigan, and we formed an instant friendship. I was preaching a Sermon series entitled 'Living in the Shadows' at the time, and Brother Dulin strongly 'suggested' that I put the messages into book form. I tried to laugh it off, but he would not let me off the hook. Each time we would get together, he would ask about the book. I finally began working on this manuscript, but to my regret, I laid it aside for a time, and he never got to read the manuscript, or make suggestions on how to improve upon it. Thank you Brother and Sister Dulin, for your friendship, and for your challenge in my life!

And finally, to all those who have shared life with me; your insights, your encouragement, and your correction (at the most critical times), have made this book both a possibility and a reality. You invested your time and your hearts in me, and I cannot thank you enough. I pray that God will bless your lives, as generously as you have blessed mine!

It was a beautiful day; the sun was shining, and the birds were singing; everything was right in the world! God had placed Adam and Eve in the garden and given them everything they could ever need. Life was simple, uncomplicated, wonderful! Then suddenly, the whisper . . . the taste . . . the fall; and for the very first time in human history, a cloud; a Shadow hung over the first couple. The Shadow blocked the sunshine of God's radiant presence and stirred something in their hearts they had never experienced before . . . fear! And the rest, as they say, is history. From that moment on, every person born into this world has come to experience the constant companionship of 'the Shadows'.

When I first began the preparation for the series of messages that have evolved into this book, I had the image of the Peanuts character 'Pigpen' stuck in my head.

Remember the little guy who walked around with a cloud (I think it was dust) over his head? That image reminds me that there is always some Shadow seeking to darken our minds, our hearts, our spirits, and even our world, as we journey toward home.

My goal in putting my thoughts on paper, is to describe a few of the Shadows that come our way, and to help the reader discover and implement God's strategy for dealing with them, so that they don't overwhelm us. While we may be required to walk through the valleys where the Shadows reside, we are never required to stay there!

I want us to start our journey through this book together acknowledging this basic but very powerful truth: the Shadows have only the life and power that we give them! There is no inherent danger . . . power . . . life . . . evil, or fear in the Shadows; those come through how we perceive, and choose to respond to them when they arise. With that in mind, let's walk together through some of life's Shadows, and discover what God has to say about them.

Living
in the
Shadows

Chapter One

Living *in the Shadow of Sin*

Since this is the first Shadow to arise in human life and history, it makes sense that we consider it first. Whoever you are, and wherever you find yourself in life's journey, you must admit that sin has, does, and will continue to attempt to cast its Shadow over you; "for all have sinned, and come short of the glory of God;" Romans 3:23.

The problem with sin is that it is such a broad topic; it is difficult to wrap our heads and hearts around. So, over the centuries, mankind has taken it upon himself to define (or should I say redefine) sin! We have managed to come up with numerous thoughts and opinions on the subject and developed a concept that allows us to label sins as 'small' or 'big'; some being worse than others. The fault in this is that it excuses or diminishes the destructive character of many of the sins among us, and so, gives us liberty to excuse some sins as being somehow 'understandable', or 'acceptable' in God's sight! Of course, the true issue with this type of thinking is that, in the Word of God, **ALL** sin is defined as sin, and **All** sin separates us from true fellowship with God!

Remember that garden scene with Adam and Eve? Once they had sinned, they felt compelled to hide (to separate themselves) from God. No longer could they walk with Him in sweet fellowship in the 'cool of the day'. Isaiah clearly tells us that "your iniquities have made a separation between you and God; your sins have hidden His face from you, so that He will not hear you" Isaiah 59:2.

There are many 'types' of sin, and each casts its own particular Shadow over us. So, let's take a few moments to consider just a few of those 'types' of sin mentioned in the Bible.

Presumptuous Sin
Psalm 19:13

Presumptuous sin is shameless sin. It 'presumes' upon God's loving mercy, and leads us to believe that we can do anything we please because God 'has to forgive us'. Consider such statements as, "I'm only human", "it's no big deal", or "God understands". While we may not give voice to these sentiments, our attitudes and actions tell all. Of course, it is the hope of every Pastor, that his or her congregation would avoid such sin in their lives. But, because of how the human nature and will operate, we aren't always on guard against the pull of our own willful, self-serving desires and passions. Along with the Psalmist, our constant prayer should be "keep your servant from presumptuous sins" Psalm 19:13.

Other Men's Sins
1 Timothy 5:22

Peer pressure has always been an issue in our lives. Why do you think Adam ate the forbidden fruit when Eve offered it to him? Everyone wants to be liked; to be a part of the group; to 'fit in'. That doesn't change just because we get older! Given the direction of our society and world today, the pressure to 'go along to get along' has never been greater. And, in spite of our assertions to the contrary, we believers are not immune to the pressure (consider Peter's denial of Jesus). Do you remember saying to your parents "everyone is going", or "everyone else is doing it"? I would venture to say that each one of us could very easily identify Peer Pressure in our workplace, in our relationships and friendships, in our extended families, and yes, even in our churches!

In civil law, a person who accompanies another in the commission of a crime, can be considered an accomplice, and can be charged for that same crime, even if they didn't 'actively' participate in the crime! While we technically may not be doing everything those around us are doing, our refusal to speak out against their actions; our 'going along to get along' identifies us as co-conspirators. We may not intend to go there, or do that, but because of Peer Pressure we could very well find ourselves becoming just like them. Remember the Bible warns us that "evil communications corrupt good manners" 1 Corinthians 15:33. In other words, choose your friends wisely, so that the Apostle Paul's instruction to Timothy "do not share in the sins of others; keep yourself pure" 1 Timothy 5:22, becomes a guideline for our future choices and activities.

Faithless Sin
Romans 14:23

I know this sounds like an oxymoron; isn't all sin faithless sin? Of course, the short answer is yes! However, there is more to consider here. Faithless sin is the sin we fall into because we fail to measure every thought, every feeling, every emotion, every desire, every word, every action and temptation by what God has to say about it. Instead, we consider only what will make us happy; what will make us feel good!

The Psalmist established a daily practice in his life that helped him to avoid sin (when he actually practiced it). We know this as Psalm 119:11 "Thy Word have I hid in my heart, that I might not sin against thee". Of course, scripture memorization alone will not prevent us from sinning, but truly understanding and applying the scripture to each and every situation will!

David knew this, but his failure to apply what he knew, led him into sin with Bathsheba. So then, if something does not stand up to the scrutiny of God's Word, *RUN*, don't walk away!

To quote a slogan from a few years ago, "just say no". Remember what Paul wrote to the Christians in Rome, "whatever is not of faith, is sin" Romans 14:23.

Ignorant Sin
Leviticus Chapter 4

Just like our children, there are times when we say or do something simply because we don't know any better! Perhaps we weren't fully or properly informed, or it may be that we aren't at the right maturity level to understand how our choices or actions violate a particular standard of God's Word. There is no 'intention' to sin, but simply a lack of knowledge or understanding.

Whatever the reason, we find ourselves under

conviction, and deserving of the consequences of our actions. While ignorance may seem to be a valid 'excuse', we can never, and must never 'choose' ignorance as a means to avoid the penalty of sin. I once had a family tell me they were going to quit coming to church because, every time they came, they felt guilty about something.

Their reasoning for staying away was that, if they didn't know, then they weren't accountable before God! Of course, their reasoning was flawed, because, choosing not to know is actually a conscious decision! Remember that, in the fourth chapter of Leviticus, we are told that sin committed in ignorance is still sin and requires the sacrifice of blood to receive forgiveness. The blood of Jesus covers our sin, but it does not excuse it!

Willful Sin
Hebrews 10:26

Willful sin is exactly what it sounds like; it is the intentional disregard for, and disobedience of God's revealed will and expectations (I choose to sin)! Of this I am certain, no truly committed and sincere child of God would enter into this type of sin.

Of all the types of sin we have examined, and all the questions we have asked over the years about the 'unpardonable sin', this comes closest from my personal perspective! God has revealed His mind to us through the writer of Hebrews, "for if we sin willfully, after that we have received the knowledge of the truth, there remaineth no more sacrifice for sins" Hebrews 10:26.

Sin of Omission
James 4:17

We can be so careful and conscious of those sins which we are tempted to commit, so focused on not 'doing' them, that we completely overlook the instruction from God to DO what is right (not just know what is right)! How much consideration have you given to the sin of omission?

All of us have metaphorically 'kicked ourselves' for sensing the Holy Spirit's direction to say or do something, and failing to do it. Most likely, we have tried to let ourselves 'off the hook' by offering ourselves (not God) some excuse, without considering it sin. We must take seriously the teaching of James when he writes "therefore, to him that knoweth to do good, and doeth it not, to him it is sin" James 4:17.

No matter what form sin takes in our lives, it is certain to cast a Shadow over us that causes us to walk in darkness rather than light; to live in fear (remember Adam and Eve hiding from God), rather than in confidence; it hinders our sweet fellowship with God who loves us so dearly, and wants to spend personal time with us. My dear reader, the Shadow of sin does not magically disappear from our lives just because we pray and tell God how sorry we are! This is a Shadow that relentlessly follows us throughout our lives, looking for any opportunity to darken our paths and steal our joy. Just as a disease or medical condition may require us to secure the services of the most qualified physician or surgeon to experience a cure; sin is a deadly disease of the heart and soul, and the only qualified source of help is the Great Physician!

Salvation is God's healing and deliverance from the deadly effects and penalties of sin; it requires of us sincere confession, and repentance of the sin committed against Him (whatever the 'type' of sin it may be); it demands an intentional turning away from that sin, with the commitment never to engage in that sin again! We must 'avoid' sin; we must 'resist' sin; we must 'flee' sin, and when we have yielded to sin, we must 'confess' that sin to God. Then, and only then can, we once again begin to walk in the light. Then we can boldly proclaim "you have cast my sins behind me" Isaiah 38:17. As you read these words, if you find yourself under the Shadow of sin, it is time to have a serious conversation with God! Come out from under sin's Shadow, into the glorious light of His presence! Then, go and take a nice long stroll with God through your garden.

Shedding the Shadow of Sin

1. Write out your personal definition of sin:

   _____
   _____
   _____

2. Write out God's definition of sin found in His Word:

   _____
   _____
   _____

3. Are your definitions the same? If not, change **your** definition!

   _____
   _____
   _____

4. Go back in this chapter and examine each type of sin; how many of these types can you identify in your life?

_____

_____

_____

5. Now . . . today . . . before you read any further:
    a. Confess your sin to God, and ask for His forgiveness and cleansing.
    b. Change anything and everything that leads you into sin (be sure to ask for God's help with this; you are going to need it to succeed).

6. Watch closely as God casts the Shadow of sin behind you; then go forward in the light of His glorious presence!

Chapter Two

Living in the Shadow of Guilt

Remember when God found Adam and Eve hiding in the garden, and asked why they were hiding? Their answer (Adam said, "I was naked, and I hid"; and "the woman you gave me, she gave me of the tree, and I ate." And Eve said, "The serpent beguiled me, and I ate.") reveals the Shadow of guilt that hung over their hearts and minds. When is the last time you felt guilty about something? For most of us, the answer to that question is "What time is it?" We feel guilty when we take the good things in life for granted, and guilty for complaining about the bad things that come our way; we feel guilty when we succeed while others are failing, and guilty for failing while others are succeeding; we feel guilty when we are doing well while others are struggling, and guilty when we are jealous of the success of others when we are struggling just to get by; we feel guilty for feeling good when someone compliments us, and guilty when others are telling us how bad we are. Are you getting the picture? Guilt is a monster Shadow that haunts our steps, and causes us to run, and yes, even to hide from God!

The prophet Hosea lamented the condition of his people, and wrote "my people are destroyed for lack of knowledge" Hosea 4:6. You see, the true danger of guilt is not that it seeks to overwhelm us, it is that we don't know what to do about it!

As I study God's Word, I discover that there are two main types of guilt at work in our lives; justified (redemptive) guilt, and unjustified (destructive) guilt. This is because there are two opposing forces at work, each with a specific purpose for the guilt.

We are told in the scriptures that, part of the work of the Holy Spirit in our lives is to 'convict' (not condemn) us; to drive us to repentance, where we can receive forgiveness and release! God uses our guilt to repair and restore our relationship with Him, so that, we don't need to run and hide. Of course, Satan has an entirely different purpose for guilt; a purpose that seeks our destruction, not our redemption. He uses our guilt as a weapon against us, hoping to drive us into the darkness of the Shadow; away from God, and into hiding. He wants to convince us that we are so 'bad' that we are beyond forgiveness; he wants to steal our peace, and the assurance that "if we confess our sins, He (God) is faithful and just to forgive us our sins, and to cleanse us from all unrighteousness" 1 John 1:9.

The key to facing and defeating guilt in our lives is first to determine where the guilt is coming from; who is at work in this guilt? Once we have answered that question, we can respond in the appropriate manner to that guilt. The starting point for this process must be the admission that we are a fallen people, living in a fallen world. In other words, 'we need help'! We might as well admit it, for God who formed and breathed life into us knows us. And yet, He still loves us! That thought never ceases to amaze me!

Let God's Spirit bring to your minds such scriptures as "while we were yet sinners, Christ died for us" Romans 5:8; "in Him (God) we have redemption and forgiveness of sins" Ephesians 1:7; "their sins I will remember no more" Hebrews

10:17, and "though your sins be as scarlet, they shall be white as snow" Isaiah 1:18! These are but a few of the many verses that instruct and remind us that God has, does, and will forgive our sins, and bring us back into right relationship with Himself. You can build your life; your hope; your future on these promises!

But, we must never forget that we have an enemy; a very powerful and determined enemy whose only mission is to steal that hope, and if possible, prevent us from finding forgiveness. Satan is a "thief who comes to steal, and kill, and destroy" John 10:10. Don't ignore this warning from the Apostle Peter who wrote "be sober, be vigilant, for your adversary the devil, like a roaring lion, goes about seeking whom he may devour" 1 Peter 5:8.

So you see, guilt can be your best friend, leading you to repentance and God's gracious forgiveness and restoration, or your worst enemy, stealing your faith and hope, and causing you to hide from God rather than running to Him! The next time guilt casts its Shadow over your life, pause and ask these two questions: "where is this guilt coming from" (who is the source), and "what is the purpose of this guilt", redemption or destruction? This will lead you to a proper understanding and response.

Everyone experiences guilt, but we don't have to let it overwhelm us, or drive us into hiding; instead, as we face our guilt, and deal with it, we can boldly and confidently proclaim "there is now therefore no condemnation for those who are in Christ" Romans 8:8!

Shedding the Shadow of Guilt

1. Does the Shadow of guilt haunt you? Do you feel like God has abandoned you? Does something in you feel the need to run and hide from God? Don't be destroyed for 'lack of knowledge'.

   _____
   _____
   _____

2. Take some time now to identify the type of guilt you are experiencing. Is it redemptive, or destructive?

   _____
   _____
   _____

3. Identify the source of your guilt. Is it God, or Satan?

   _____

_____

_____

4. Write out a personal prayer asking God's forgiveness. Ask Him to restore you to a right relationship with Him.

_____

_____

_____

God is always true to His Word, and always keeps His promises . . . trust Him to defeat Satan . . . again!

Chapter Three

Living in the Shadow of Fear

Adam and Eve were 'afraid' of God's presence there in the garden; Abraham was afraid he would die without an heir; Joseph was afraid he would be forgotten in prison; the Israelites were afraid the Egyptian army would destroy them, and later, afraid they would die of hunger and thirst, and they were afraid of the giants in the land they were going through and to (the land God had promised to give them); the disciples were afraid of the storm, and later, of being arrested and executed for being followers of Jesus; the thief on the cross was afraid of dying without hope; and today, many believers are afraid of what God might ask or make them do! Just like guilt, fear is always close by, looking for an opportunity to darken our hearts, and minds and lives.

Do you find it interesting that fear was born in a 'perfect place' . . . the one place it should never have existed? And It all began with one bad decision. Of course, this world is far from perfect! Our world is filled with fear; that's why Psychologists and Psychiatrists; authors and speakers; doctors and medical laboratories are making billions of dollars each year attempting to help people 'cope' with their fears. The problem is; no counselor, no book, no public speaker, no physician or pill producer can truly conquer fear. But God can! Consider these lessons on fear found in God's Word:

Fear is not God's plan for our lives
2 Timothy 1:7

Early in my ministry, for a variety of reasons, I began to experience panic attacks. I could literally feel them coming on. My breathing would become rapid and shallow; my heart felt like it would beat right out of my chest; I would break out in cold sweats, and get so dizzy I had to sit or lie down to keep from fainting. And, the more symptoms I had, the greater my fear became! It was during one of those 'spells', when I didn't know what to do, that I finally turned to God and His Word for answers (sound familiar?). It was then God directed me to His promise that "God has not given you a spirit of fear" 2 Timothy 1:7. That is when I finally realized that there were other forces at work in my life besides God!

Long story short, as I began claiming that promise to my life, the fears began to subside; in just a few months (I wish I could say it was sooner) the panic attacks were gone. I haven't had another attack since! This wasn't some 'magical' solution to my problem, it was simply the application of God's Word to what was happening in my life. Whatever you fear, I can tell you for certain that it isn't coming from God, and it is not His will that you be a prisoner of that fear. Why not do what I did; claim the Word of God as your source of strength and peace, and His promise as your 'security blanket'. Then, watch as the fear begins to dissipate, as God's truth destroys Satan's lies!

Fear is contagious
Isaiah 8:12

In an earlier chapter, I quoted the old proverb that "bad

company ruins good morals"; it will also rob you of peace in your life. All around us, people are living in fear. If we are not extremely attentive and cautious, we could contract the disease just by being around others who have it. How else would you explain good, committed followers of Christ living in fear of economic collapse; of Y2K, of the end of the world, etc.? Isaiah saw this in his day, and cautioned the people "say ye not a confederacy, to all them to whom this people shall say, a confederacy; neither fear ye their fear, nor be afraid" Isaiah 8:12.

Remember this, fear drove Adam and Eve to step away from the comforting presence of God; to separate themselves from the one who could banish fear and restore peace and calm to their lives. Fear will have the same effect on our lives if we don't assert God's controlling Word when this Shadow begins to rise over us!

The best way to avoid fear is to stay away from those who live in its Shadow, and seem to be under its control. Instead, maintain close fellowship with those who live and walk in the peace and confidence of God's abiding presence.

Fear is natural
Psalm 56:3

This may sound like a contradiction to what I have previously stated, however, because of what happened in the garden, fear is now a part of our 'natural' existence in this world. The Psalmist wrote "what time I am afraid, I will trust in thee" Psalm 56:3. Did you catch that? He said, "when I am afraid" not "if I am afraid". You see, like any other problem we face in life, the first step toward victory is to admit we have a problem. Do you remember when you first made Christ your Savior? You first had to admit that you had a sin problem, and were in need of Saving? This is true of all the Shadows I am sharing about in this book.

In my introduction, I made this statement, "the Shadows have only the life and power we give them". I am restating that principle here when I say that, 'it is not the existence of fear that is our problem, it is the power we permit fear to exert over us that is the problem.' While there are a few 'healthy' fears that benefit us in life, most fears seek to destroy us. They accomplish their purpose when we allow fear to override our better instincts of faith. Think for a moment about the story of the disciples in the boat with Jesus when the great storm hit; several of them were veteran fishermen, who had been caught in violent storms before (these were normal occurrences on the Sea of Galilee). Yet, on this night, instead of facing their fear, they surrendered to it! This is why Jesus asked them "why are you so fearful"? Mark 4:40. My friend, remember this, if God is in your boat, you have nothing to fear from the storm. You need simply hold on to His hand (to your faith) and ride out the storm. The Word of Peace is coming your way! Yes, fear is 'natural', but it is not normal for the one whose faith is in God!

Most fears are borrowed Psalm 53:5

This principle builds on the fact that fear is contagious; once we get the bug, it spreads through our 'systems' very rapidly, and affects our 'thinking'. Some years ago, I ran across some staggering statistics concerning fear. I want to share them with you, to help you get a clearer picture of what fear can become and do if we give in to it. According to those statistics: 70% of everything people fear will never happen; 22.5% of everything people fear could happen, but probably won't; 7% of everything people fear will happen, but there is nothing they can do about it, and 5% of everything people fear is worth fearing! What these numbers tell us is that, most people are 'fear borrowers'; we let fear come in and take up residence in our lives! Fear is like a computer virus, once it gets into the system, it spreads and corrupts all other programs. Do you think this might have been what Jesus was trying to address in Matthew 6:34 when He said, "Take therefore no thought for the morrow: for the morrow shall take thought for the things of itself, sufficient unto the day is the evil thereof" ? In other words, stop borrowing fear, justified or not, from tomorrow, and letting it ruin your today! The Psalmist got it right, and described the problem perfectly, when he wrote "they were in fear, where no fear was" Psalm 53:5.

There is always an 'exit' from fear
Psalm 34:4

    Do you remember the lyrics to a song from a few years ago "'God will make a way where there seems to be no way"? Fear tells us that there is no way out for us; that we are its prisoners, under a lifetime sentence; that God can't or isn't going to help us this time. Of course, this is a lie, but we tend to believe it anyway. However, this is not what God says! God says that He will always make a way to deliver us out from under life's Shadows; and that includes the Shadow of fear!

    Do a character study of your personal heroes of the faith in the Bible, and you will discover two basic truths about every one of them: first, you will discover that they all lived under the Shadow of fear from time to time; second, you will see that, as they looked to God, and cried out to Him for help, that He always made a way out for them. Don't just take my word for it, check it out for yourself. God has promised to save and deliver us from all our fears, if we let Him. We need to follow the example set by the Psalmist, who experienced his own share of fears in life, but was able to write "I sought the

Lord, and He heard me, and delivered me from all my fears" Psalm 34:4.

    Several years ago, in our Wednesday night Bible study, we spent time examining the Book of Ecclesiastes . . . what some refer to as 'Solomon's Diary' of his search for life's meaning and purpose. During that search, one of the truths he discovered was that "fears are in the way" Ecclesiastes 12:5. We can understand and apply this insight to our lives in two distinct ways: first, we can interpret these words to mean that, as we journey through this temporary earthly life, fears are going to make appearances; we aren't going to be able to avoid or go around them, we are going to have to face them because they are a part of our 'normal' life experience; but, we can also take this verse to mean that, if we aren't paying close attention, we may find ourselves tripping over fear; it becomes a stumbling stone seeking to block our path; to get 'in the way' of experiencing the presence and power of God in our everyday lives!

    As I mentioned before, I am not ignorant of how fear operates, nor am I immune to its Shadow effect; I understand that almost everything about living carries within it the potential for creating fear in us; but, when God is near, fear loses its power! God has instructed us "fear thou not, for I am with thee: be not dismayed for I am thy God: I will strengthen thee, yea I will help thee" Isaiah 41:10!

Are your fears paralyzing you; limiting you; preventing you from experiencing the true peace of "God with us"? Then, do something about them; take God at His Word; put Him to the test, He really doesn't mind 'showing off' in our lives when we give Him the opportunity!

Shedding the Shadow of Fear

1. What do you fear right now? Make a list of all your fears, large and small in the space below:

   _____
   _____
   _____

2. Does God want you to live in fear? How do you know?

   _____
   _____
   _____

3. Try to identify when each fear began: where were you . . . what were you doing . . . who were you with . . . is this your fear, or is it borrowed?

   _____
   _____

4. Go back to the statistics concerning fear listed in this chapter and apply the proper statistic to each fear listed.

_____

_____

_____

5. Look for God's exit from fear; ask Him to show you what you cannot see with human eyes; Remember . . . "God will make a way where there seems to be no way!"

Say goodbye and good riddance to the Shadow of fear!

Chapter Four

Living in the Shadow of Doubt

I hope that, as you have been reading, you have come to understand that the 'Shadows' of life never truly leave us; this is not a once and done affair! Fears are always waiting for the next circumstance, the next problem, the next opportunity to once again cast their dark pall over our lives.

The fourth Shadow we need to consider then, is the Shadow of Doubt. The Webster's Dictionary defines doubt as 'to question the accuracy or validity; an unsettled state or condition'. I prefer the Vine's Expository Dictionary of New Testament Words, which defines doubt this way: to question; to be perplexed to the point of anxiety and desperation; to be without a way. Isn't this exactly what the Shadow of doubt does? Isn't this the way doubt makes us feel . . . alone, desperate, drifting without a rudder to steer with? Have you ever considered that our doubts are actually an accusation against God; that doubt questions God's desire or ability to keep His promise? This is exactly what doubt does, and why Satan loves to raise this Shadow over our lives! In fact, you could say that doubt is a 'limit switch' on what God will (not can) do in our lives. Consider what happened in Nazareth: Jesus had returned to his hometown to minister, but the people would not believe that he was who he said He was. The scriptural account reveals the effects and consequences of their doubt; "they were offended at him, and . . . He could do no mighty works, save He laid hands upon a few sick folk, and healed them. And He marveled at their unbelief (doubt)" Mark 6:3-6. What 'great things' have we missed out on because of our doubt? More importantly, why do we doubt? There are many possible reasons, but let me quickly offer just five found outlined in the Bible:

Fear
Luke 24:38

In the previous chapter on fear, I mentioned that fear is a 'natural' but not normal experience for the believer. Of all the things we might fear in life, God should certainly not be found anywhere on that list! And yet, on a certain day shortly after his death, when the one the disciples had declared Him to be Messiah, the one they had called Lord stood in their presence, fear was their first response. Why? Because of doubt! They couldn't wrap their heads around the idea that Jesus was actually standing there, in the flesh. They had watched as He was arrested and led away; they had seen Him die on the cross; they knew exactly where He had been laid in the tomb, guarded by Roman soldiers. It was done, over, he was gone! Doubt had crushed their hopes and dreams, and yes, even their faith. They feared what they could not understand; does any of this sound familiar? Does any of it make sense? Haven't you seen that, when fear casts its Shadow over your life, the Shadow of doubt is its close companion? Perhaps you need to hear again the words Jesus spoke on that day "why are ye troubled? And why do thoughts (doubts) arise in your hearts?" Luke 24:38. It's the same question we must answer today . . . "why do we doubt"?

Divided loyalties
Matthew 6:24

Over and over again, the Israelites walked under the Shadow of doubt; over and over again, God would chastise them, and remind them that their hearts were not wholly His! But let's not judge them too harshly, after all, it's not an easy thing to put God first in everything; it's not easy to say no to activities and events that interfere with church attendance; it's not easy to say no to our children when their social or sports activities are scheduled on Sunday or Wednesday; it is never easy to set aside our own will to do what God asks of us! But, if our hearts and minds are truly set on putting God first, there will come times when these 'choices' are set before us. We will be required to decide . . . to choose. Will we, like the Israelites, have divided loyalties?

What activities, what recreation, what relationship, what home or family responsibilities are calling you to 'divide' your loyalties? The Bible reminds us of Jesus' words "no man can serve two masters: for either he will hate the one, and love the other; or else he will hold to the one, and despise the other. Ye cannot serve God and mammon" Matthew 6:24. Will you choose to serve the Master who gave His only begotten Son for you, with all your heart, and mind, and soul, and strength? Will you be able to say with Joshua "as for me and my house, we will serve the Lord" Joshua 24:15? If we continue to divide our loyalties, we are inviting doubt to be our constant travelling companion!

Lack of focus
Psalm 10:4

When our loyalties are divided; when we are overloaded, the natural consequence is that we lose the ability to properly focus on the task at hand. In the time and culture we live in; where multitasking seems to be close to a religion in itself, it seems our call is to become 'jugglers' rather than disciples! There are so many voices, so many schedules, so many needs, so many responsibilities competing for our attention, what are we to do?

In Psalm 19:7-11, the Psalmist passes along to us the very hard fought, and slow learned process he used to restore his focus . . . the 'practice' of centering his thoughts and actions on knowing and serving God. And, do you remember how God expressed His feelings about this?

God said, "I have found David, the son of Jesse, a man after mine own heart, which shall fulfill all my will" Acts 13:22! We must continually be asking ourselves, "What does God think about this, how can this job . . . this duty . . . this activity . . . this relationship . . . these thoughts serve and glorify God who created me to reflect His image, and carry His name?" You see, the key to focus is prioritizing; centering our thoughts and actions on what is truly most valuable and important; not from an earthly perspective, but from an eternal perspective! I am discovering that, when I do this; when I center my thoughts on God; when I keep His will as my top priority, it equips me to make better choices and decisions; to complete the tasks of life that matter most, and have eternal value. If I fail to do this, then these words from the Psalmist haunt my thoughts: "the wicked, through the pride of his countenance, will not seek after God; God is not in all his thoughts" Psalm 10:4.

Poor choices
Isaiah 7:9

We have all been guilty of this in our lives. How many times have we mentally kicked ourselves, and asked "why did I do that", or "why did I say that", or "why did I go there", or "why did I make that choice or decision"? Most of our poor choices can be traced back to a lack of belief. I know this is a bitter pill to swallow, but consider this: if I choose anything not in balance with what God says, do I typically try to excuse or rationalize that choice by saying, "It's not all that bad" or "I'm sure God understands"? The difficult truth is that, I know neither of these statements are true, or acceptable to God, no matter how much I want them to be! Think about this for a moment; if we truly believe God means what He says; that the Bible is the inspired and infallible Word of God, then we really shouldn't be making choices or decisions that we have to try to justify, or explain away! And, if we don't make poor choices and decisions, then we don't have to try to minimize our regrets. And, when we don't have to live with regret, doubt can't cast much of a Shadow over our lives or linger too long!

I don't know about you, but the words Isaiah spoke to King Ahaz, "if you will not believe, surely you will not be established" Isaiah 7:9 make me want to make better choices! If we are honest with ourselves, and with God, we must admit that doubts do come to us. It will serve us well to do regular and honest evaluations of our decision-making process, and then, to bring that process into harmony with what we profess to believe.

Distractions
Matthew 14:30-31

This may be the most subtle, and dangerous of all the 'giants' we face as we seek to live for God. How many appointments do you have today; this week; this month? What 'extra' work have you been assigned at your job? How many trips will you make transporting kids, or others, to activities and events? How many loads of laundry need to be done? How tall is the grass? How dirty is the car? When did you last pay your bills, or balance your checking account? Are you getting the idea? Our lives are extremely busy, and while each of these 'things' may be important on some level, they can also easily distract us from what is 'most important', loving and serving God with all our hearts, and all our minds, and all our strength; in other words, putting Him first!

When Jesus invited Peter to join Him out on the water, Peter immediately responded and stepped out of the boat because he believed he could do it; after all, Jesus had called him to come! Those first few steps must have been truly exhilarating! Can't you just imagine Peter looking back to those other men still in the boat, and saying "Hey fellas, look at me"? But then, it happened; he felt the wind blow hard against his face; he saw the waves building higher and higher; and then, he began to sink; "but when he saw the wind boisterous, he was afraid; and beginning to sink, he cried out saying, Lord, save me" Matthew 14:30. What happened? He got distracted, he started thinking about the storm, instead of keeping his focus on Jesus, and what he had been called to do! The story continues, "and immediately Jesus stretched forth His hand, and caught him, and said to him "O thou of little faith, wherefore didst thou doubt"" Matthew 14:31. That's the million dollar question isn't it? What has caused us to doubt?

What happened between the moment we surrendered our lives to Christ; proclaimed our undying and unwavering love and commitment; promised to put him first in everything, and this 'sinking' feeling we have now? The answer is simply 'we got distracted'. Could it be that, if we would simplify; if we would downsize, if we would prioritize and put our focus back on God, the Shadow of doubt would have to move? Distraction causes confusion; confusion leads to chaos, and chaos always carries us back under the Shadow of doubt.

As I have previously stated, these are not all the factors that could, and most likely will contribute to our becoming distracted, and finding ourselves blanketed by the Shadow of doubt, but they are a good starting point for us to begin evaluating and adjusting; and when we do that, we can walk out from under doubt's Shadow. And the good news is that, even when we doubt Him, God doesn't give up on us! He didn't let Peter drown; He brought him safely back to the boat; He brought the Israelites into the Promised Land; He invited Thomas to reach out and touch the scars; and, He inspired the writers of the Bible, to put it all down in black and white. He did all this so we could refer back to all His promises and interventions when our times of doubt come! My friend, take God at His Word, and remember, "don't be of a doubtful mind" Luke 12:29.

Shedding the Shadow of Doubt

1. In what areas are you most prone to doubt?

_____
_____
_____

2. What 'causes' of doubt do you most identify with?

_____
_____
_____

3. What are you afraid of?

_____
_____

_____

4. Where are your loyalties?

_____
_____
_____

5. How focused are you? What (Who) is your focus on?

_____
_____
_____

6. What is your process for decision making?

_____
_____
_____

7. What distractions do you need to deal with?

_____
_____
_____

Remember, if God is not Lord <u>of</u> all, He is not Lord <u>at</u> all!!!

Chapter Five

Living in the Shadow of Bitterness

Bitterness, like so many other 'conditions', is actually a heart problem. When it casts its Shadow over our lives, not only do we walk in the darkness it casts, we tend to 'absorb' some of that darkness; it blackens our hearts, and minds, and spirits, and souls! Bitterness is best defined as 'anger, disappointment, or resentment over some actual or 'perceived' unfair word, situation or treatment' in our lives. Bitterness is often very slow growing; like a cancer that goes undetected until it becomes a serious problem, perhaps even terminal! Do you recall the story of the experiment involving a frog, and boiling water? It was discovered that, when a frog was thrown into a pot of boiling water, it immediately jumped out of the pan to safety; but, when that same frog was placed in a pot of cool water that was slowly heated to the boiling point, the frog stayed in the pot and was boiled to death! This is how it is with bitterness in our lives; if we grow too comfortable with it, eventually it will kill us (at least in the spiritual sense). This is why the writer of Hebrews cautions us to "look diligently lest any man fail of the grace of God, lest any root of bitterness springing up trouble you, and thereby many be defiled" Hebrews 12:15.

Did you notice the writer's reference to the 'root'? It doesn't take much for bitterness to find a place to grow in our lives. It can begin with an unkind word spoken to us; a betrayed confidence; a broken promise; a small misunderstanding; a perceived slight, or even just a 'look'! Suddenly, we find that things are not 'sitting well' with us, and the seed has been sown.

Do you fight the yearly battle with crabgrass and dandelions that I do? I have tried just about every method I have heard of to get rid of them when they make their presence known; I have even tried digging rather large holes around them, trying my best to get all the root, and still, they come back! The explanation seems to be that, if even a 'mustard seed' sized piece of the root remains, those persistent weed will continue to haunt us, and defy our best efforts eradicate them! But, there is a solution, it is called 'pre-emergent' application. In simple terms, if we treat the problem before it is a problem, then we can better control the unwanted weeds in our lawns. Bitterness is just like those weeds; just when we think we have won the war, those weeds just pop right back up at the most unexpected, and unwelcomed times! Bitterness could very well be (and most often is) a symptom of other underlying issues in our lives; it could also be the full-blown disease that threatens our spiritual (and possibly physical) health. Where many of the sins we have to deal with, such as anger (I have a chapter on this later in the book), are rather quickly, and sometimes destructively diagnosed and expressed, bitterness is usually internalized; kept hidden; unnoticed, festering like an undiscovered wound.

Several years ago, I went on a Mission Work Camp to Thailand. The wood there was very coarse, and difficult to work with (pulling splinters often took more time than the project we were working on); a few years later (yes years) I discovered a swelling and tenderness on the top of my leg. I went to see a Dermatologist, and, after an examination, she told me there was something under the skin that needed to be removed. As soon as she made a small incision, the 'problem' popped right out . . . it was a tiny sliver of wood I had unknowingly brought home with me from Thailand. It was surprising to me that it had gone unnoticed for so long, but had finally festered, and needed attention.

This is exactly what happens with bitterness. That tiny 'root'; that 'splinter', lays hidden until, all of a sudden there it is, causing a problem, and needing immediate treatment! None of us is immune; we are created as emotional beings, and bitterness is just that, an emotion. An emotion we don't want to claim; an emotion we don't want to admit we have or could possess. As believers, we tend to believe we should just be able to 'refuse admittance' to this emotion, and it will disappear. Obviously, we are wrong!

Jesus knew this Shadow would pop up in our lives from time to time; that is why He prepared us for those moments with these words: "be of good courage, I have overcome the world" John 16:33. And that 'overcoming' includes human emotions!

By now, you may be asking the question "How do I

know if there is a root of bitterness in me?" Try answering a few questions with me: Do I tend to be more negative than positive with the people around me? Do I own a 'grudge collection'? Do I tend to see life more about me, than about others? Do I feel that everyone and everything is out to get me? Do I feel cheated about the way my life has unfolded? Am I a cynical person? If you have answered yes, or even maybe to any of these questions, there may be a 'root of bitterness' in you that needs attention!

In Exodus, Chapter 15, we find a section covering the travels of the Israelites in the wilderness, on their way to the Promised Land. In this chapter, they find themselves having gone three days without water (apparently their provisions have run out). They finally arrive at a pool of water located there in the wilderness, anticipating a long, refreshing drink to quench their thirst; but to their disgust, they find the water bitter and undrinkable. As I read the stories covering their travels, I find this is just one more in a long line of challenges and disappointments for them. So, in essence, finding the water undrinkable becomes the 'final straw' for them; bitterness wells up within them, and they grumble and complain. And then, God does what He always does; what He does best; He shows up and provides a solution (a tree) to their current problem. Once the tree is thrown into the pool, the water becomes fresh and drinkable.

God used another tree to 'freshen' our lives; to get rid of the bitterness that springs up in us; that tree held the body of His Son, our Savior . . . the one who makes life fresh and new! Have you taken a long drink from that refreshing pool? You see, the treatment for bitterness is not all that complicated; admit there is a problem (we are thirsty and bitter), we call that confession; ask for help (we can't make the water fresh ourselves), we call that repentance; then, in the forgiveness He gives, let the bitterness go, (we call that Redemption)! I didn't keep that little sliver of wood in my leg for a souvenir; I didn't need or want to be reminded of that experience. Don't hold on to even the memory of bitterness when the 'Great Physician' has removed it for you!

Peter rightly diagnosed this problem in Simon the Sorcerer, (the story can be found in Acts, Chapter 8), when he said to him "I perceive that thou art in the gall of bitterness, and in the bond of iniquity" Acts 8:23. No matter how good we think we are at hiding or covering up the bitterness that has cast its Shadow over our lives, there is someone who knows it is there. In fact, there are two who know it exists in us: we know it (even if we try hard not to admit it), and of course, God knows it is there; we can't hide anything from Him!

If you find, as you read these words, that there is any 'root' of bitterness in you, no matter how small or insignificant it may seem, why not pray right now, the prayer the Psalmist prayed when he found himself falling short of the best he had to offer God: "create in me a clean heart (free of all bitterness), O God, and renew a steadfast spirit within me" Psalm 51:10.

Bitterness is a 'learned condition', we aren't born with it. It is a negative response to a difficult or unfair circumstance in life. And, just as we learn to be bitter, we can learn to let go of bitterness (with God's help of course). If you won't do it for yourself, do it for your children and grandchildren! It is proven that bitterness can be passed on to succeeding generations; don't you want to be the one to break the cycle? In conclusion, let me encourage you to declare "I can be bitter or better, . . . I choose better!"

Shedding the Shadow of Bitterness

1. Begin by asking God to search the hidden places of your life, and to reveal any 'bitterness' found there.

   _____

   _____

   _____

2. Identify the circumstances, and the individuals who have sown the seeds of bitterness in your heart; be specific . . . make a list:

   _____

   _____

   _____

3. As you identify the people, places, circumstances that create bitterness, forgive them! Remember forgiveness is for YOU, not for them!

_____

_____

_____

Finally, intentionally let go of bitterness; picture it leaving in your mind; then, watch the Shadow of bitterness depart! Now, take a long, refreshing drink of the 'water of life' and move forward!

Chapter 6

Living in the Shadow of Unforgiveness

I recently read an article that stated "forgiveness is probably the most difficult thing we do". Would you agree with that statement? Have you ever struggled to forgive someone who has said or done something to hurt you, or someone you love? Then you are one of the millions of us who proclaim ourselves to be Christians, yet struggle to get out from under the Shadow of unforgiveness.

The Bible Dictionary defines forgiveness as: 'giving up the right to vengeance (revenge/getting even). Forgiveness is not a 'feeling', it is a 'mindset'; it is a conscious act of the will, and it takes a lot of prayer, preparation and practice to get anywhere close to being good at it!

Let me share just a couple of insights right here about what forgiveness is **not**! First, forgiveness is not forgetting what someone has said or done to hurt you or cause you harm. Our minds are designed by God to store everything in our memories, so it is all 'up there' somewhere, just waiting for the right 'trigger' to be released back to our conscious minds. Second, forgiveness is not denying the injustice that has been done or letting someone 'off the hook'; it is not letting them 'get away with it'! And finally, forgiveness is not some magical incantation or potion that we can use to dissolve or ease the pain we feel.

Do you realize that forgiveness doesn't require the interaction of two or more parties to happen? Forgiveness simply requires each of us to act like Christians are called to act; to be the Christians we profess to be; to surrender our 'right' to get even, and inflict pain in return; to let go of the emotion involved in the situation!

This brings us to the subject of this chapter . . . unforgiveness! Again, the Bible Dictionary defines unforgiveness as 'the deliberate decision or refusal to give up our right to vengeance'. A closer look reveals unforgiveness to be a major 'character flaw' (at least as it appears in Christian living); one that almost always (probably always) results in the Shadow of bitterness 'tag teaming' us! One Shadow is bad enough, but combining these two makes things even darker, and seemingly more impossible to overcome.

As we consider the Light of forgiveness, and the Darkness of unforgiveness, we have contrasting stories from the Bible to illustrate each response: Joseph's story is found in the Book of Genesis, Chapters 37-50. His story points us very clearly to the picture of forgiveness that we want to be our picture! Joseph was hated by his brothers (for various reasons, some of which we might consider valid); thrown into prison for something he didn't do, and forgotten by a former cellmate he had helped. If anyone had a right to be bitter and un-forgiving, it is certainly Joseph! Yet, as you read his story, you will never find the Shadow of unforgiveness manifesting itself in or through his life or actions. When he is finally released from prison, he doesn't berate his former cellmate for forgetting him; when his brothers show up in Egypt in need of food, he gives it to them; when he finally reveals his identity to them he doesn't make their lives miserable (which they expect and deserve), he forgives them and weeps at the opportunity to be reconciled to them.

On the other hand, we have the story of the Prodigal son, found in Luke's Gospel, Chapter 15. I sometimes think this is more accurately the story of the 'Prodigal' brother! After all, he is the 'poster child' for the spirit of bitterness and unforgiveness! When his brother returns home after squandering his share of the inheritance, the 'Prodigal brother' can't find any place in his heart for forgiveness and reconciliation; he won't even enter the house! The fact that their father welcomes his brother home is bad enough, but when he had the 'fatted calf' killed and prepared; puts a robe on his back, and a ring on his finger; throws a 'welcome home' party, and reinstates him into the family, the 'Prodigal brother' is angry; jealous; vengeful; he has no intention of 'celebrating'! What I find interesting about this story is that, the 'Prodigal brother' was not the one who had been wronged; it was the father who had been betrayed! Yet, it was he who harbored the spirit of vengeance; it was he who had the Shadow of unforgiveness clouding his heart and mind.

Let's take some time to consider a few of the reasons

people tend to entertain unforgiveness in their hearts: First, they refuse to forgive because they don't 'feel' like forgiving. I wonder if this is how Peter was feeling when he asked Jesus "Lord, how oft shall my brother sin against me, and I forgive him? Till seven times?" Matthew 18:21. How much is enough? How many times do I have to let him 'get away' with it? Don't those sound like reasonable questions; questions you and I might want to ask? Second, there is the 'feeling' that, if we forgive (especially more than once) we are just condoning their action; that in fact, they are 'getting away with it', and we are letting them! I don't know about you, but I have certainly felt that way when God asked (actually commanded is a better term) me to forgive. What I fail to remember is that, judgment is God's department, not mine; and He has said that He will execute judgment in His way, and in His time. What He asks, and requires of us, is that we trust Him, and stay out of His way. Third, forgiveness is difficult because we simply don't 'want' to forgive; what we want, is for them to feel the same pain we are feeling; to have a dose of their own medicine!

The idea, at least in our heads, is that, if they experience this pain, they won't do that again (probably not the case). Finally, forgiveness is difficult because we have been taught, in one way or another, that to truly forgive, we must first forget! I covered that point earlier, but let me say that, if I keep remembering and rehashing what has happened, I probably haven't truly forgiven and let it go. On the other hand, since, as I stated before, our minds are programmed to retain everything, it would be virtually impossible to truly forget. I don't believe God is asking us to go through some form of 'mind erasure' procedure; what I do believe is that He is asking us to forgive, and to let go of the 'emotional energy' tied to the situation; to reject any 'feelings' which tend to lead us toward some type of 'getting even'. So then, how are we going to get past these areas of difficulty, and banish the Shadow of unforgiveness from our lives; and how are we going to know when we get there? A successful strategy should look something like this: Step one . . . remember, and take seriously what Jesus said about forgiveness "if ye forgive men their trespasses, your heavenly Father will also forgive you; but, if ye forgive not men their trespasses, neither will your Father forgive your trespasses" Matthew 6:14-15. It sounds to me like God takes this forgiveness business very seriously! Step two . . . we need to confess our struggle with unforgiveness, and ask for God's help. We all know that we can't do it without His assistance. We have proven that more than once in our lives! Step three . . . begin to honestly and earnestly pray for those we need to forgive "but I say unto you which hear, love your enemies, do good to them which hate you, bless them that curse you, and pray for them which despitefully use you" Luke 6:27-28. Jesus understands how hard this is for us, so he modeled it for us from the cross when he prayed "Father, forgive them, for they know not what they do" Luke 23:34. And finally, Step four . . . take out the trash; "let all bitterness, and wrath, and anger, and clamor, and evil speaking be put away from you, with all malice; and be ye kind, one to another, tenderhearted, forgiving on another, even as God, for Christ's sake has forgiven you" Ephesians 4:32.

In my research for this topic, I ran across this very appropriate quote: "forgiveness is a gift; not a gift you give to others, but a gift you give yourself" (author unknown). Give yourself the gift of forgiveness, and the peace and contentment that accompanies it, and rejoice as the Shadow of unforgiveness disappears from your life!

Shedding the Shadow of Unforgiveness

1. List all the people and circumstances you are having difficulty forgiving: You may need an extra sheet of paper:

   _____
   _____
   _____

2. Revisit the list of reasons why forgiveness is so challenging:

   _____
   _____
   _____

3. From your list above, number them 1 to . . . with one being most difficult, and in descending degrees of difficulty; then apply the Four Step process to each one,

until you have eliminated each one from the first list on this page.

_____
_____
_____

Remember, forgiveness is a choice, a conscious act of the will!

Once you have completed this exercise, say goodbye to the Shadow of un- forgiveness, and hello to peace and joy!

Chapter Seven

Living in the Shadow of Greed/Covetousness

Have you ever found yourself jealous of someone's success, position, popularity, possessions, or even their health? Have you ever asked, "Why can't I have that . . . do that . . . go there . . . own that?" Or perhaps, in order to soothe or diminish the conviction that often accompanies this type of thinking, you attempt to 'spiritually sanitize' your feelings by saying "I wish I had (you fill in the blank), and he/she had something better? If so, then you have already had some experience with the Shadow of greed/covetousness!

Greed is defined as 'an intense, selfish desire for something' (usually having to do with wealth, power or possessions); covetousness is defined as 'wanting what someone else has' often expressed by a 'whatever it takes' approach to getting it. And all facts point to both of these conditions being insatiable; or, simply put, even if we get what we want, we probably won't be satisfied! The story is told of a young reporter interviewing the late Howard Hughes (at that time, he was believed to be the richest man on earth); and the reporter asked him "Mr. Hughes, how much is enough?", to which Mr. Hughes replied, "just a little bit more". By the way, Howard Hughes died as a very rich but unhappy recluse; and his wealth and power could do nothing about it!

In an article written by Andrew Greely, and published in the April 5, 2019 edition of the Chicago Sun Times, Mr. Greely stated that, "the most serious spiritual problem in the country today is greed"; and he pointed to the political, sports, entertainment and corporate arenas to support those claims. We have seen how Pharmaceutical companies hold people hostage to high priced medicines; watched the ever increasing prices of products related to the oil industry; seen the exorbitant salaries athletes are demanding to 'play; we are constantly given peeks into the lavish lifestyles of Hollywood actors and actresses; and our heads reel as we hear the latest number of dollars being raised by political candidates! But, the worst part is that most of us just shrug our shoulders and say, "Oh well, if they can get it, more power to them!"

Can you remember when our society was defined by its charity, and concern for the welfare of others? How did we get from there to where we are today? The answer to that question is not complicated, it is that greed/covetousness have become the 'norm'; they have brought us to the place where our first question is "what's in it for me'? But, even though we have come to accept such attitudes and behaviors as normal, the Mental Health experts define this type of thinking and acting as 'abnormal'; even they know this is not how we are created to live and function. Do you see the irony in that?

Consider the sad truth that, shortly after creation, the sin of greed (also known as covetousness in the Bible) reared its ugly head. Read Genesis, Chapter 3: God placed Adam and Eve in the garden, and given them everything to enjoy and experience. His only exception was the Tree of the knowledge of good and evil. Then, Satan shows up, and points their attention to the one tree (not all the others); he accuses God of being selfish, and cheating them out of 'something they deserved to have': "God doesn't want you to have the 'very best' (my paraphrase)! That got Eve's attention, and scripture records that "when the woman saw the tree was <u>good for food</u>, and that it was a <u>delight to the eyes</u>, and that it was <u>desirable to make one wise</u>, she took from it and ate" Genesis 3:6. The fruit was . . . good . . . a delight . . . desirable.

If you will do an in-depth study on this topic, you will discover at least three ways we are tempted to greed/covetousness, and how they impact our lives. First, our judgment becomes impaired (we begin to make unwise choices and decisions); second, our ethics become compromised (we tend to accept attitudes and behavior we previously rejected); and finally, we begin to justify and rationalize our actions (everyone is doing it)! Look again at the story in the garden; do you see how these temptations played out in that first scenario? Greed/covetousness are not new additions to human history, we have simply taken them to new extremes; Satan accuses God of being unfair, and tempts us to sidestep what God says, in favor of what we want!

The prophet Jeremiah penned these words concerning the conditions he saw in his day: "everyone is greedy for gain"

Jeremiah 6:13. Even King David, the man 'after God's own heart' was pulled in: in the 11th Chapter of Second Samuel, we find the record of David 'lusting' for Bathsheba. He knew she was married to one of his soldiers, but used (abused) his power as king to have her brought to his bedchamber, and slept with her while her husband was away at war! Then, when she told him she was pregnant with his child, he tried to cover his 'tracks' with several attempts at deception; and when those failed, he had her husband murdered! You see, the problem with greed/covetousness, as with all forms of sin is that, once we have fallen under its Shadow, we find ourselves engaged in even worse conduct to keep it hidden. No wonder the 'Shadow of greed/covetousness is so dark and ominous!

As you do a quick self-examination, are you detecting any warning signs that greed/covetousness is at work in our life? One point that needs to be made here is that greed/covetousness are acts of the human will; you see, we still have the power given us by free will' to resist, or to yield to the temptation that assaults us. There are so many verses in the Bible dedicated to this issue, and instructing us to 'prepare ahead of time' for these temptations so that we are able to recognize this Shadow as it begins to rise over us. Consider these few verses: "thou shalt not covet your neighbor's house . . . wife . . . servant . . . cattle . . . nor anything that is thy neighbor's" Exodus 20:7; "he that loveth silver shall not be satisfied with silver, nor he that loveth abundance with increase" Ecclesiastes 5:10; "take heed, and beware of covetousness; for man's life consisteth not in the abundance of the things which he possesseth" Luke 12:15, and 'for the love of money is the root of all evil; which, while some coveted after, they have erred from the faith, and pierced themselves through with many sorrows" 1 Timothy 6:10. Can you recall the story of the rich young ruler who came to Jesus and asked "what must I do to inherit eternal life"? When Jesus moved past the young man's 'good works', and instructed him to sell all he had, give everything to the poor, and "come follow me", the young man went away sad, because he couldn't bear to part with his many possessions Mark 10:17-31.

Are you seeing the big picture here? Greed/covetousness are very serious problems, and we need to be on guard against them at all times! This is a huge Shadow to try to work our way out from under. The best strategy, of course, is to avoid it altogether. But, if we discover ourselves already blanketed by its Shadow, there are some specific steps we can take to correct our attitudes and actions: first, take inventory; we must do a very thorough, and brutally honest search of our hearts, and identify any desires that have led us to this place; next, change course (remember God allows **_you_** turns); confess our failures to God and acquire His forgiveness, and seek the help of the Holy Spirit to avoid or resist future temptations in these areas; then, determine if our environment (family, job friends, co-workers, acquaintances etc.) contribute to our attitude of greed/covetousness, and make any and all necessary changes to stay in God's favor and out of the Shadows; and, finally, learn to appreciate what we already have (I was praying this morning, and thanking God for all the blessings I enjoy, and realized how rich I truly am); look at the blessings God has poured out so abundantly in your life, and say with the Apostle Paul "I have learned, in whatever state I am in, therewith to be content" Philippians 4:11. Contentment is our 'super weapon" to defeat the spirit of greed/covetousness when it arises. When (not if) we get to this place; this condition; this attitude of living, the Shadow of greed/covetousness will be dispelled like the morning mist, and we will live free of the guilt and shame of being so easily drawn in!

Shedding the Shadow of Greed/Covetousness

1. Are you battling the Shadow of Greed/covetousness? List some the things you might 'want' that could open you up to greed/covetousness.

   _____
   _____
   _____

2. How much is enough?

   _____
   _____
   _____

3. How is your judgment? Are the choices and decisions you are making good and wise?

_____
_____
_____

4. How are your ethics? Have they changed to fit society's norms?

_____
_____
_____

5. How are your actions? Are they justified by God, or by you?

_____
_____
_____

6. If God asked you today to give up everything you own, could you/would you do it?

_____
_____
_____

7. Can you say right now "I am content with what God has

given me"? If you can honestly answer yes, congratulations, the Shadow of greed/covetousness has no more power over you!

Chapter Eight

Living in the Shadow of Lust

Lust is defined as: 'a strong, intense, often uncontrollable desire for something' (usually sexual in nature). I would venture to say that most Christians would quickly and emphatically state that lust is not an issue for them. Some of this may be due to a faulty definition, or understanding of lust; some may be a denial of any actions or attitudes that might be perceived to be lustful; some denial comes from a strong and determined effort to keep it hidden! If we have learned nothing else in our journey through this book, I hope we can agree that nothing is ever truly hidden from God. In fact, in the Bible He reminds us "for nothing is secret, that shall not be made manifest; neither anything hid, that shall not be known abroad" Luke 8:17.

Lust in its fully expanded definition will take one of two specific forms: the first is 'material lust', which we have covered in the previous chapter; the other, more pronounced and familiar form is physical and sexual lust. In this chapter we will focus our attention on the physical/sexual lust that can tempt us to try to hide in its darkness!

First, would you agree with me that lust springs from our human desire for 'self-gratification': our desire to 'feel good'? Physical/sexual lust is the most selfish of all sins; it refuses to take into consideration any effect or consequence that affects others (I'm not hurting anyone but myself); but, in all honesty, it is just all about pleasing myself! Physical/sexual lust makes the one desired simply an 'object' for my pleasure; it dehumanizes and depersonalizes God's highest creation, (men and women). I know that some will argue that 'looking but not touching', is not really lust, but let's take a look at what Jesus had to say on this topic: "anyone who looks at a woman (or man) to lust after her (him) has already committed adultery with her (him) in his (her) heart" Matthew 5:28. Lust is a powerful and deadly enemy; that is why James wrote to believers, "each one is tempted when they are drawn away by their own evil desires and enticed. Then, when desire has conceived, it gives birth to sin, and sin, when it is fully grown, brings forth death" James 14:15. I would express it this way; lust permitted into our minds, becomes lust birthed in our hearts; lust in our hearts, leads to sinful behavior; sinful behavior leads to separation from God, and separation from God ends in eternal destruction, and spiritual death!

The challenge lust presents is that it, or at least its influence, is all around us; consider the magazines you see in the racks at every checkout counter; advertising for a multitude of products and services; just about every TV show (including those promoted to be 'family friendly'); most Hollywood productions, and even the music of our day, and you can easily identify some element designed to appeal to our physical and/or sexual desires! And it is not limited to those 'worldly' folks around us, it is a major problem in (not just for) the church as well. Here are the latest statistics: more than 40 million (yes, you read that right) people of both sexes visit Porn sites every year . . . 70% of youth Pastors report at least one of their youth struggling with Pornography . . . 68% of church going men, and 50% of Pastors report viewing Pornography regularly . . . 59% of Pastors report married men in their congregations seek help with battling Pornography; * there are, as of this writing, 42 million Porn sites, and 370 million pages of Pornographic material available on the internet; * 47% of families identify Pornography as a problem in their home; * the viewing and use of Pornography increases the marital infidelity rate by 300%, and 56% of divorces are directly related to the use of Porn . . . 33% of young men and women report searching Porn sites at least once a month; and the statistic that most concerns me, *the average age our children are exposed to some form of Pornography is 11 years old, and 94% of our children will have viewed some form of Pornography by the age of 14! Do these statistics concern you as much as they do me? Oh, by the way, these same statistics show the viewing and use of Pornography among Christians and Ministers to be the same as those outside the church!

Oh yes, my dear readers, lust is a big problem in the Church! So then, if lust is such a big problem, how do I know if it's **my** problem? And if it is, how can I get out from under its Shadow? Let's begin with some identifying characteristics best expressed in question form: What is my thought life like? What do I allow myself to see, think, feel, do? When I see a woman (man) provocatively dressed, what is my first response; where does my imagination take me? How dominant are thoughts of a sexual nature? How much time do I spend thinking about, or viewing programs, websites, magazines and TV, movies, or any other materials that stimulate physical desires or feelings? Do I tend to rationalize these with such statements as "I'm only human" or "it doesn't hurt to look"? Do I ever consider how these thoughts and feelings could affect others? Is it really 'all about me'? If you can identify with even one of these as being a 'part' of your life, then "Houston, we have a problem"!

Of course, the good news is that, "there hath no temptation taken you, but such as is common to man: but God is faithful, who will not suffer you to be tempted above that ye are able; but will with the temptation, also make a way to escape, that ye may be able to bear it" 1 Corinthians 10:13. This has become one of the primary weapons in my arsenal, to defeat temptation in all its forms! To help dispel the Shadow of lust in our lives, there are specific steps we can (and must) take: we can avoid the people, places and things that stimulate our fleshly desires . . . "I will set no evil thing before my eyes" Psalm 101:3; we can think higher thoughts . . . "let all things be done for edification (building up) 1 Corinthians 14:26; we can change our dress . . . "put on the full armor of God" Ephesians 6:11-18 (this must include shedding our 'wordly' dress); we can adjust our thought life . . . whatever things are true . . . honest . . . just . . . pure . . . lovely . . . of good report, think on these things" Philippians 4:8.

If you have ever done any hard physical work, you know that, over time, your hands become calloused (there was a time I could stick a needle into the callous, and never feel pain) . . . lust is like that; it comes in so innocently, so subtly, that it goes unnoticed until, like all forms of addiction, it requires more and more to be satisfied; we become desensitized to its harmful effects in our lives. Just a little harmless fun, we tell ourselves; then, when the damage is done, we see the true effects our sin has had on our family, our friends, our church, our relationships (especially our relationship with God); we feel trapped and overwhelmed! But, we are reminded that God has made a way to escape! So, I believe there is a proper approach we can take to defeat this powerful enemy whose name is lust.

First, you need to approach this problem from a practical standpoint. It will be absolutely necessary for you to be brutally honest with yourself. You may have done such a good job of 'covering your tracks' that no one around you has even a hint that lust is an issue in your life. But, *YOU* know, and even more importantly, God knows! Remember, you cannot hope to resolve a problem that you haven't first admitted exists, and needs attention. You will need to do some serious and extensive housecleaning as well. It is imperative that you begin by getting rid of any and all printed materials in your possession (books, magazines, pictures, even advertisements such as calendars, etc.), that create or feed lustful thoughts, feelings and actions in you! If you are serious about defeating the lust that is warring within you, you must begin to eliminate all sources of lustful thoughts, feelings and desires. Then, you must move on to your websites (personal, work and 'private') that you have access to (I believe that it is possible to block these sights, and prevent them from appearing again). And, you must commit to refusing to open any email or notifications that may appear from these sites in the future! Next, examine the company you keep (friends, co-workers, acquaintances, even family); do any of them encourage, support, condone or join you in lustful thoughts or actions? If so, you will need to sever all ties with them. If you don't take this step, you will find yourself being drawn right back into the sin you are seeking to conquer in your life. I know this as a recovering alcoholic. It is a painful process to be sure, and they won't understand, but, like a cancer, you must eliminate the sources of the disease to be free from it! Finally, get counseling. This may be the most difficult step of all because it requires you to admit to another person (don't use anyone you know personally) that you have this problem. I promise you that if you try to go it alone, the odds are stacked against you; you will most likely try to justify or minimize the sin; even rationalize it away, or you will simply try to 'manage' the lust that controls you! Of course, my suggestion is that you seek out a Christian counselor who will include scripture and prayer in their approach and plan.

As I have already stated, these are 'practical' steps you can use to begin your recovery from lust. But, to truly defeat the monster Shadow of lust, you will need a courage; a strength; a power that you cannot generate on your own; you will need God's help above all else! So, along with the practical steps you can take, you must also take spiritual steps to experience complete victory in your war with lust. But first, I need to say that, the proclamation of our 'humanness' must never become an excuse for immorality. Just because a thought, desire or feeling is natural, doesn't mean that it should be considered normal! We are constantly reminded in

God's Word that the natural man (human nature) is in constant conflict with the spiritual man (redeemed nature). Satan wants to rob us of the spiritual grace, peace, freedom and victory we are entitled to. John, in his Gospel, points us to Jesus' words, when He said "the thief comes only to steal, and kill, and destroy; but I have come that they might have life, and that they may have it more abundantly" John 10:10. If we are battling the sin of lust in our lives, we are not living the 'abundant' life' Jesus was talking about! Rather, we have given control over to our human nature; "every man (person) is tempted when he is drawn away by his own lust" James 1:14.

The good news in all of this is that God has prepared a way out for us; the door to that 'way' is 'self-examination'. When John wrote "you will know the truth, and the truth will set you free" John 8:32, he was not just speaking of the truth of Jesus' divinity and ministry; he was also speaking of the truth of our own sinfulness that leads to conviction, confession, and the freedom God's forgiveness can and will bring into our lives! When we are willing to face, and accept the truth of who and what we are in our sinful condition, then we are prepared and free to become who and what we are supposed to be by the grace and power of God's transforming work in us! That is why He said "my grace is sufficient for you, my power is made perfect (perfectly revealed) in weakness" 2 Corinthians 12:9-10.

Are you ready to take on and defeat the lust that has been controlling you? Are you prepared to offer your body as a 'living sacrifice' for God's use and service? Do you long to experience the 'abundant life' that Jesus has planned for you? Then don't wait another moment; begin today to let His transforming power be unleashed in your heart, and mind; in your body and soul!

Here are the steps to full surrender and victory:

- **Confess** your sin, and ask for God's forgiveness
- **Request**, and **permit** God to change your thought processes
- **Eliminate** as many I's (self) from your conversations with God and others as possible, and get rid of everything that stirs the sin of lust in you
- **Search** the scriptures (there are many) for the weapons

God has made available to you in your war against Satan and his influence in your life

- **Believe** God's promise that "if we (you) confess our sins, He is faithful and just to forgive us our sins, and to cleanse us from all unrighteousness" Romans 8:1
- Finally, my friend, make this little chorus your daily prayer and desire: "Lord, prepare me to be a sanctuary, pure and holy, tried and true; and with thanksgiving, I'll be a living sanctuary for you"!

Now, dear reader, watch the Shadow of lust fade from your life as God gives you the victory that has become your heart's true desire!

Shedding the Shadow of Lust

1. Are you fighting a battle with 'lust'; have you, or are you trying to justify or minimize your lustful thoughts and actions? Can you, will you now admit that your lust is damaging your relationship with God (and perhaps with others)?

   _____
   _____
   _____

2. Answer the questions concerning lust posed above; do you have a lust problem?

   _____
   _____
   _____

3. Do you consider your lust to be 'natural' or 'normal'?

_____

_____

_____

4. Will you now confess to God that you have a lust problem?

_____

_____

_____

5. List all sources, people, places, materials that feed your lust; then take the steps outlined in this chapter.

_____

_____

_____

6. Now, center your thoughts, actions, attitudes and desires on God and His will for your life.

7. Start singing the chorus 'Lord, prepare me to be a sanctuary, pure and holy, tried and true; and with thanksgiving, I'll be a living sanctuary for you'. If you don't know the tune, U Tube it, or simply speak the

words daily as a prayer!

Watch God work as He transforms your heart and mind, and say goodbye to the Shadow of lust, it cannot dwell in God's wonderful presence!

Chapter Nine

Living in the Shadow of Death

Do you remember the lead into the Star Trek shows, "Space, the final frontier"? I want to say right here and now that they got it wrong. Space is not the final frontier, death is! Death is the greatest 'unknown' of all; perhaps the darkest of all Shadows that fall over our lives. The fear and dread of death springs from not knowing what will happen when we die (not just to ourselves, but to our families), and from not being properly prepared.

Somewhere in my reading I ran across this quote, and wrote it down thinking I would someday use it in a sermon. I must apologize to the writer for not making a note of his/her name, but this quote speaks to the real issues of life and death, as nothing else except the scriptures can; "a person is not ready to live, who is not first ready to die". Do you understand the great wisdom in those few words? How many people go through life never truly living, because they aren't ready to die? I hope to make the Apostle Paul's words my theology for life; he wrote "for me to live is Christ, and to die is gain" Philippians 1:21.

Psalm 23 is one of the best known and most quoted of all scriptures, right up there with John 3:16. The Psalmist faced some of life's most challenging and difficult situation with a peace that astounds us. How did he do that? What was his secret? He shared his secret with us when he wrote "yea, even though I walk through the valley of the Shadow of death, I will fear no evil, for thou art with me" Psalm 23:4. As you can see, the Psalmist had a 'Preparedness Plan' in place for every situation, including dying!

I live within a few miles of a Nuclear powered electrical generating station. Once a year the utility company sends out a manual entitled 'Emergency Preparedness Plan' to all household in the surrounding communities. On the last Wednesday of each month, the Emergency Management

System sounds the warning sirens to test the 'readiness' of the system (I pray nothing happens on the last Wednesday of the month because we are so used to the siren on that day that no one pays it much attention).

Every family is encouraged to prepare a personal 'disaster plan'; a strategy for the possibility of a nuclear emergency. The plan is to include an escape route; a designated meeting place for all family members in case of separation; the location of the nearest emergency shelter, and an emergency supply kit. All of this, 'just in case' something happens. It might not, but it could! Doesn't it make sense then, for believers to put as much time and effort into creating a 'preparedness plan' for life and death? Death is not a 'possibility', it is a 'certainty'; we will all die! Would you allow me to offer you some basic truths to help you 'prepare' for death?

Everyone dies
Ecclesiastes 3:19

There it is, the cold hard truth of life; "it is appointed once unto man to die" Hebrews 9:27! Death will come to us all unless the Lord returns before that 'appointed' time comes. But then, because that is true, death is no more to be 'feared' than birth! Have you ever considered why we celebrate when a baby is born, but fear and grieve when someone we love dies, and is 'born into eternal life'?

I will admit that there was a time in my life when the thought of dying struck a chord of fear in me; but over the years, God has stilled that fear with the awareness that, physical death is simply the natural consequence of physical living: "to everything there is a season, and a time to every purpose under the heaven: a time to be born, and a time to die" Ecclesiastes 3:19. But, thank God, we are not trapped in this physical dimension! Guy Penrod captures this thought in a song on one of his albums: "a soul rises up to heaven, another little baby's born"; we call this the 'cycle' of life. Death may be inevitable, but it is also our gateway into God's eternal presence where death no longer exists! Don't let the fear of death distort or rob you of this truth and hope.

Fear of death is bondage
Hebrews 2:15

Fear of dying can become a chain that holds us in the prison of grief and despair. It can prevent us from experiencing the peace and joy that only God can give us, in the saddest times of life. This fear fuels a multi-million dollar industry that offers everything from surgery, to 'magic pills'; from age defying creams, all the way to cryogenic preservation of our dead bodies, in the hope of being 'brought back to life' later! The writer of Hebrews reminds us that Jesus became flesh, and lived and died, to "deliver them who, through the fear of death, were all their lifetimes subject to bondage" Hebrews 2:15. It is time we faced our fears concerning death, and allow God to prepare us to 'live'!

Not everyone dies 'on time'
Ecclesiastes 7:17

Many Christians have been deceived into believing a concept that is not supported by Scripture: we have come to believe that every time a person dies, from the stillborn baby, to the murder victim; from the one killed in an auto accident, to the one who dies of a heart attack, or some disease, that it was 'their time' to die. While there are certainly some instances where this may be so; the truth is that, not all deaths are an 'act of God' . . . not every death is the result of an 'appointed time on God's calendar. There are actually deaths recorded on 'death certificates' where the cause of death is listed as 'accidental', or' murder', or 'suspicious circumstances', or even 'undetermined'. Knowing that death could come at any time, could cause us to live too 'carefully'; it could also free us to live more 'courageously', and more focused on our mission for Christ! I don't know about you, but knowing death is unpredictable, inspires me to "walk circumspectly, not as fools, but as wise; redeeming the time, for the days are evil" Ephesians 5:15-16. The reality that death will come, greatly reduces the 'trivial pursuits' that can often become the routine of my life. Consider this counsel from Solomon: "be not over much wicked, neither be thou foolish; why shouldest thou die before thy time?" Ecclesiastes 7:17.

For many years, I have heard the saying "saints die well", but it has taken me most of my life to figure out what this really means. Now that I have, when I consider the question "how will I die", it has nothing to do with timing, and everything to do with answering the question "has my life had a spiritual impact on those I leave behind"? It is no great feat to die; everyone is going to do that; but to leave a witness; to leave a memory, a trail for others to follow that leads to Christ and eternal life, now that is a great way to live and die! Consider once again the quest of Solomon for understanding in the book of Ecclesiastes; answer the question he poses to us all: "how does the wise man die?" Ecclesiastes 2:16.

Life outlasts death
John 11:25-26

This is the ultimate truth that takes the "sting' out of death, and the 'fear' out of dying! To know that death is simply the exchange of 'mortal life' for 'eternal life'; to know that Jesus keeps His promise (I go to prepare a place for you); to know that death is not the end, this makes life worth living! When I was a boy growing up in Pennsylvania, the grocery stores where we lived gave S&H stamps with every purchase. When we filled enough books with the stamps, we could 'redeem' them for merchandise. As we live our lives each day, we are gathering 'stamps' that will someday be 'redeemable' in God's eternal kingdom! There is not only comfort, but great anticipation in these words Jesus left us: "I am the resurrection and the life. He who believes in me, though he were dead, yet shall he live; and whoever lives and believes in me, shall never (truly) die" John 11:25-26. You see, if we truly believe what Jesus said, then we 'know' that a new life, a better life, is waiting for us just on the far side of the Shadow of death.

Like the caterpillar that wraps itself in the 'tomb' of a cocoon, death becomes our moment of 'transformation'; it calls us to spread our wings and fly! And it is all because of what Jesus has done and is doing in our lives. When He conquered death, He handed us the key that unlocks the door between mortal and immortal; between perishable and imperishable; between the temporary and the permanent (check out 1 Corinthians 15:53-57).

We must be ready
Matthew 24:44

The chorus of an old Christian hymn cautions us to "be ready, be ready, be ready when He comes". The key to successful and fulfilling living, is to be ready at any moment to die. If we put the same effort and energy; yes, even the same money into living, that we do into trying to 'cheat' death, imagine the kind of life we could have while we are here! Imagine the testimony we could leave behind!

Are you beginning to see how 'freeing' it can be not to have the 'worry', or the 'fear' of death hanging over our heads and hearts; casting its dark Shadow over what should be joyful and abundant living? Of course, this means we must shift our priorities, and our focus, so that we are properly preparing ourselves to live; both in the here and now, and in the eternal kingdom to come. Jesus warns us to "be ye also ready, for in such an hour as ye think not, the Son of Man cometh" Matthew 24:44. When we are completely prepared to die; when the fear of death no longer hold us in bondage, then life can truly happen!

The ultimate goal
Numbers 23:10

I work for a Funeral Home here in our community, and I spend a good amount of time in cemeteries. Have you ever walked through a cemetery, and read the epitaphs on the tombstones? It can be quite enlightening; sometimes saddening; but often quite inspiring! Believe it or not, I have given some serious thought to what I would like my inscription to be. I don't care if it is actually 'chiseled in stone' as long as it is etched on the hearts and minds of those I leave behind . . . "he lived . . . he died . . . a righteous man". I want to die 'right' in the sight of God! I want to live in a way that pleases Him, and I want to die with a testimony of a life well lived according to the standard God sets in His Word. I want my final prayer to be "let me die the death of the righteous" Numbers 23:10. Let me say this one more time before moving on: the secret to dying well, is to live well; and the secret to living well, is to be prepared to die!

If you haven't figured it out yet, I will repeat it one more time; the Shadows have no real life or power other than that which we give them! Even the Shadow of death is an illusion; an illusion of loss, of separation and loneliness; an illusion that can create fear in us, only if we allow it to!

The prophet Amos gives this advice to all who, sometime in their lives (usually more than once), makes the journey through the valley of 'death's Shadow'; "seek Him whom turns the Shadow of death into the bright morning" Amos 5:8

So you see; even death is simply a Shadow! It has no power except the power we give it. But if we have a 'preparedness plan' in place, we have all we need to move beyond the Shadow, into the light! Have you made a 'preparedness plan' for living, and dying? If not, why not lay this book aside for a time, and develop that plan right now; it will make all the difference between existing, and really living!

My dear readers, come out from under death's Shadow; bask in the warmth of God's abiding presence; then boldly proclaim, "thanks be to God who gives us the victory through Jesus Christ our Lord" 1 Corinthians 15:57.

Shedding the Shadow of Death

1. Do you fear death? Can you explain why?

   _____

   _____

   _____

2. Does your fear of death prevent you from living your best life?

   _____

   _____

   _____

3. Do you have a 'Preparedness Plan' for living and dying?

   _____

   _____

4. If you knew you would die tomorrow, what would you do today?

_____
_____
_____

5. What do you want your testimony; your epitaph to be?

_____
_____
_____

6. Start taking all the necessary steps to ensure that your 'legacy' will outlive you.

Now go experience the life you were created to have; walk free from the Shadow of death!

Chapter Ten

Living in the Shadow of the Almighty

So far, all the Shadows we have been considering are the Shadows we spend a lot of time, money and energy trying to avoid or outrun. We admit that these Shadows will come and go repeatedly throughout our lifetimes; and, sometimes they will even threaten to overwhelm us. But, there is a Shadow we seek; a Shadow we long to dwell under; a Shadow that creates a place of comfort, and peace, and safety; a Shadow we run *to*, not *from*. It is the Shadow of God Himself!

If you are a fan of the Psalms, as I am (you have probably figured that out), you can find some real insights into how we can best 'abide' under His Shadow. Consider just a few of these are outlined for us in Psalm 91:

Dwell
verse 1

To dwell, means to stay; to take up residence; to spend extended periods of time. One thing you will discover about the Shadow of the Almighty is that, it is so large no other Shadow can compete with or overshadow it! In other words, to quote a favorite chorus of mine "my God is so big, so strong and so mighty, there's nothing my God cannot do"! Now, that's a big Shadow! And, when we are dwelling there, we are free from the fears and uncertainties created by all those other Shadows. If we must 'dwell' somewhere, let it be 'under the Shadow of the Almighty'!

Trust
verse 2

Trust God; hold to his unchanging hand; He will not let you fall! Trust is the <u>glue</u> that keeps us connected to the Almighty. It is the <u>force</u> that forms the Shadow under which we can abide. Trust is the <u>key</u> that unleashes God's awesome, life changing, heart changing, circumstance changing power in our lives! When we trust, we no longer "lean on our own understanding" Proverbs 3:5. Our trust is expressed best when we don't understand, but simply accept that 'God is working everything out in His own time, and in His own perfect will and way', and that is good enough for us! Do you see how trust in the Almighty generates peace, which is the exact opposite of fear and doubt?

Truth
verse 4

Over the centuries, mankind has wrestled with the concept of truth, only to arrive at the question "what is truth"? The problem is that, from human perspective, all truth as we know it is 'subjective'; each person's truth may be (often is) different from another's. And so, truth becomes a relative term, too easily thrown around and manipulated, in order to be used as an excuse to do whatever 'feels right'.

The Psalmist does not speak of his own truth, or the truth of his society, or culture, or social group; he speaks of 'absolute truth'; truth spoken by the very lips of God Himself! That truth, proceeding from God, will always be 'the truth, the whole truth, and nothing but the truth'!

Unfortunately, being human has its disadvantages. We are surrounded and bombarded by the 'world's' truth; our' mind's' truth; our 'emotion's' truth; our 'peer group's' truth; our 'employer's' truth; our 'friend's' truth . . . etc. So, how are we to find and know what is 'real truth'? The answer is not as difficult as it seems, or as we sometimes make it. If God said it, or inspired it to be written down for us in the Bible, then it is true enough to build our entire lives; our hopes and dreams; even our eternal future on! All other truth is limited, biased, and flawed. Under the Shadow of the Almighty, "ye shall know the truth, and the truth shall make you free" John 8:32!

Love verse 14

There should be no question in our minds that God loves us; we are told that "God so loved the world that He gave His only begotten Son" John 3:16. His Son died in our place.

One of the first songs I learned and sang in church after I was saved was 'I should have been crucified'; the first lines read "I was guilty, with nothing to say, and they were coming to take me away; but then a voice from heaven was heard that said, "let him go, and take me instead"; and I should have been crucified, I should have suffered and died; I should have hung on that cross in disgrace, but Jesus, God's Son took my place". I still have a hard time understanding why God loved me that much, don't you?

But the real question here, the biggest question of all is, am I returning that love? Before you answer, you might want to ask yourself "how much, and how well do I love God"? Do I love Him enough to do His will when it clashes with mine? Do I love Him enough to set aside quality time to be with Him? What sacrifices am I willing to make; what price am I willing to pay (this is not just about money), to prove my love for Him?

The Psalmist records how God responds when we love Him with "all our heart, and soul, and mind, and strength": "because he has set his love on me, I will deliver him, I will set him on high" Psalm 91:14. Under the Shadow of the Almighty, is a delivering and elevating love _we_ long to experience, and

He longs to provide!

Call
verse 15

The longer we dwell under His Shadow, the more comfortable our conversations with Him become. The closer we draw to Him; the more we trust Him, the more we pour out our true thoughts, and feelings, and struggles to Him. Suddenly, we discover that we don't just want to go to Him with the 'big things' in life, we want to discuss even the smallest details and annoyances with Him. We want to know what He thinks; how He feels; what His plans are for us! Hear again what God has to say about our calling upon Him: "he (you and I) shall call on me, and I will answer him; I will be with him in trouble; I will deliver and honor him" Psalm 91:15. God, as our heavenly Father, wants us to call upon Him like His children (that's what He calls us); to share our struggles and concerns with Him. Are you calling upon God today, and every day?

Satisfy
verse 16

Are you 'mature' enough to remember the Rolling Stones singing "I can't get no, satisfaction"? That is certainly **_not_** the song we should be singing, is it? Under the Shadow of the Almighty is complete satisfaction! In Him we find perfect balance; perfect peace; what Paul wrote of as 'contentment'. Here is the harsh but necessary truth: Outside of a relationship with God, you will never have enough money; enough time; enough friends; enough success; enough popularity; enough possessions; enough health, or beauty, or even enough years to be completely satisfied! But, under His Shadow, we can find the same satisfaction the Psalmist found: "with long life I will him satisfy him, and show him my salvation" Psalm 91:16. Oh yes, there is perfect satisfaction; it comes from Him who is 'enough'!

Dwelling in the Shadow of the Almighty

1. Are you right with God? Can you dwell in His presence without guilt or fear? If not, take care of that right now. Invite Him to be your Savior and Lord!

   _____
   _____
   _____

2. Are you dwelling in His presence?

   _____
   _____
   _____

3. Are you trusting Him to keep His word?

   _____
   _____
   _____

4. Do you live in His truth, and not your own?

_____
_____
_____

5. Are you returning the love He has poured out in your life?

_____
_____
_____

6. Are you calling upon Him; seeking His counsel in all things?

_____
_____
_____

7. Are you finding the true satisfaction that can be found in Him?

_____
_____
_____

Isn't it a wonderful thing to dwell under the Shadow of the Almighty? Take a few moments now to thank Him for all He is, and all He has done, and all that He is going to do in your life!

I hope you realize that, in my small efforts to identify and provide some insights into the Shadows that plague us in life, that I haven't come close to naming or discussing all the Shadows we will face. I would encourage you to dig deeper; to go further in discovering what God has to say about such other Shadows as loneliness; discouragement; despair; anger; gossip; backbiting; carelessness; apathy; ignorance, and so many others. This is a journey that will take a lifetime; a journey worth the taking; an effort worth making! It won't be easy, or comfortable, but it will lead you into a deeper and more loving relationship with the only one in whose Shadow we can truly say "it is good to dwell here"!

And so, as I draw this book to a close, let me share one final earth shattering, life changing insight with you: in order for there to be a Shadow, there must first be a source of light! As long as you set the light behind you, you will always be walking into the Shadow; but, when you set the light before you, the Shadow must move behind you! Jesus said, "I am the light of the world" John 8:12; the Psalmist knew what he was talking about when he stated, "I have set the Lord (the light) always before me" Psalm 16:8.

Has He, is He casting His light before you? Does He go before you, causing the Shadows to fall behind you? Let us respond to the invitation of the prophet Isaiah, "Come let us walk in the light of the Lord" Isaiah 2:5! When we abide under the Shadow of the Almighty, His light will cast away all other Shadows. The Shadows of Sin, Guilt, Fear, Doubt, Bitterness, Unforgiveness, Greed and Covetousness, Lust, and yes, even Death must fall away! Then, we can walk and live in the joy, and the peace, and the victory of His presence, now and forever!

Amen

www.ingramcontent.com/pod-product-compliance
Lightning Source LLC
LaVergne TN
LVHW051841080426
835512LV00018B/3006